Written and Illustrated by

Anthony F. Monterroso

First Edition

ISBN: 1542599695
ISBN-13: 978-1542599696

I dedicate this book to my wife and children. They have inspired me to continually create and push myself to do better.

-Anthony F. Monterroso

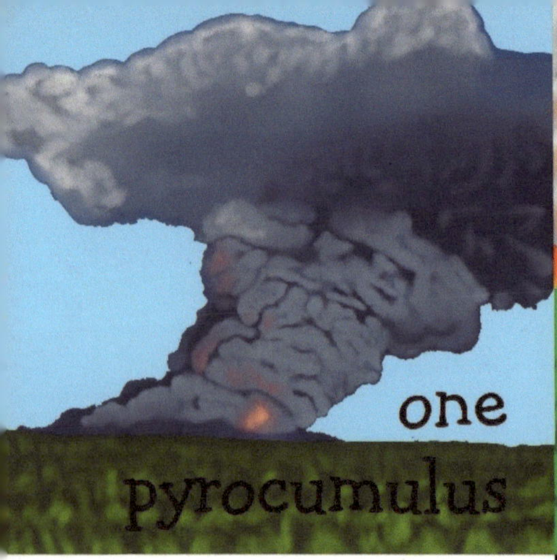
one
pyrocumulus

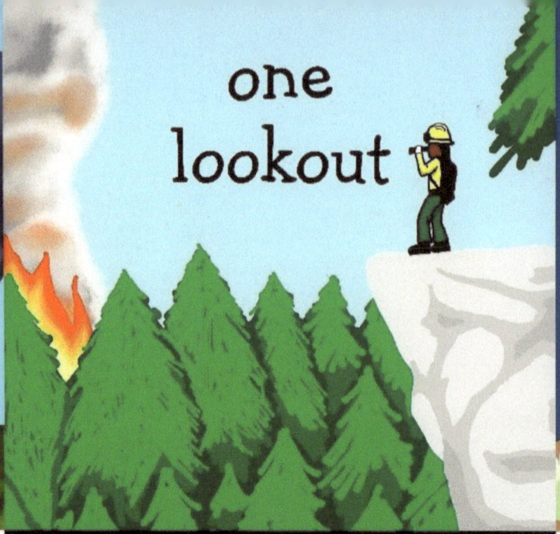
one
lookout

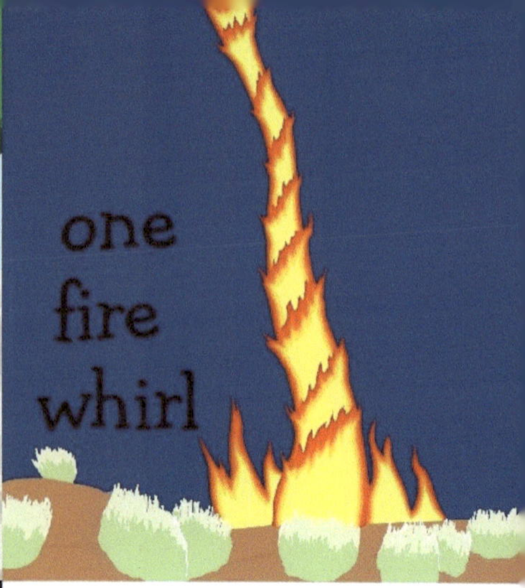
one
fire
whirl

Can you use your hands like binoculers?

1

What color is the tent?

one
tent
z
z
z

one
sleepingbag

one
torching
tree

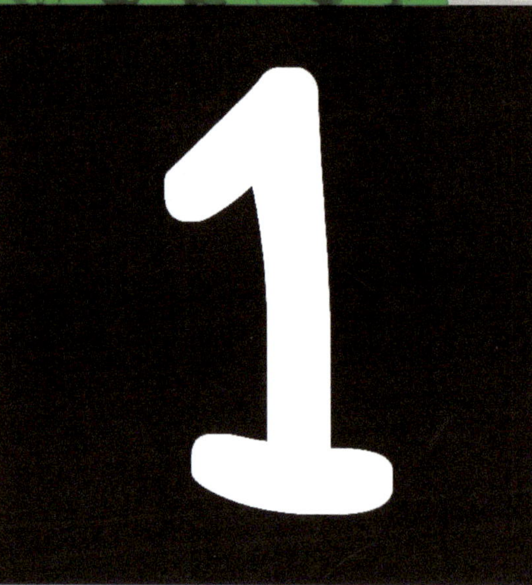

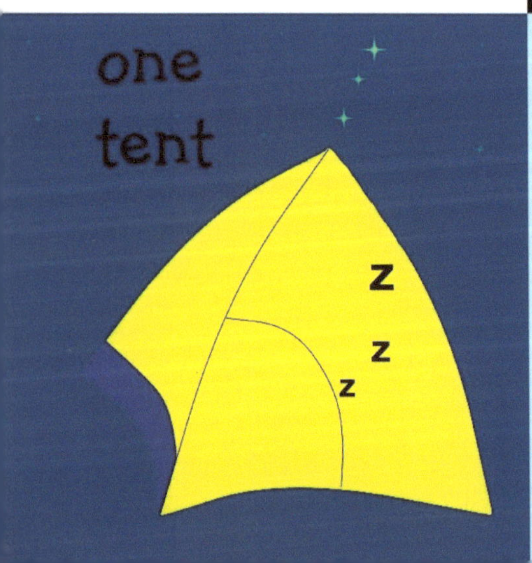

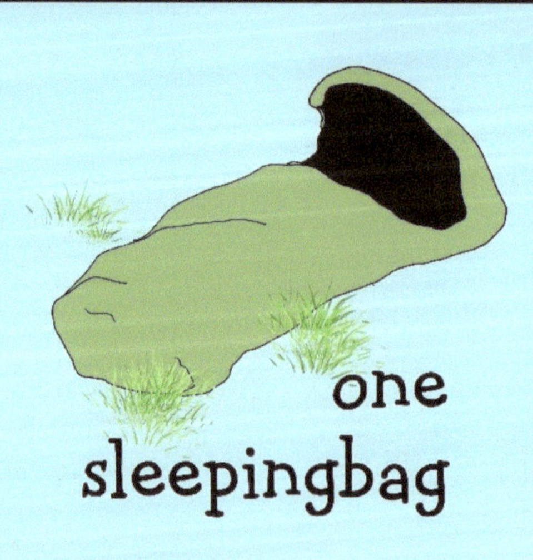

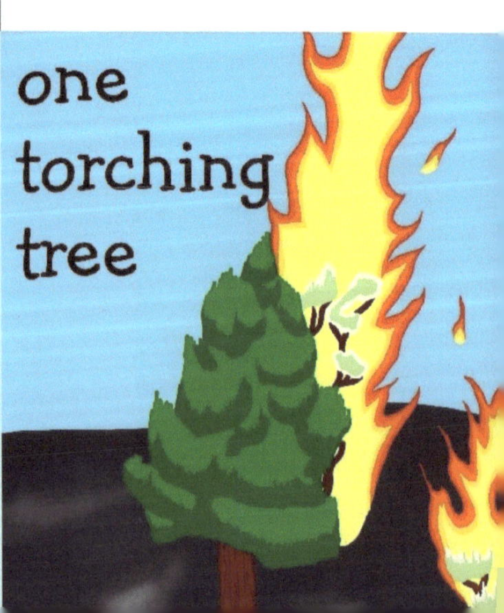

PETROL
BAR OIL
PETROL
BAR OIL
two gas/ oil cans
two falling axes
two wedges
Can you sound like a chainsaw?
2
Which firefighter is the sawyer?
two sigs
two chainsaws
two firefighters

three type
3 helicopters
554
554
554
three type 1
helicopters
three
type 2 helicopters
What
helicopter
has the
most blades?
3
What
bucket is
the largest?
three
rappellers
three
short-haulers
three buckets

four dozers

four crew buggies

four type 3 engines

What color is the Type 5 engine?

What sound does a siren make?

four type 5 engines

four ambulances

MEDIC UNIT

four command trucks

five adjustable barrel nozzels

five foam nozzels

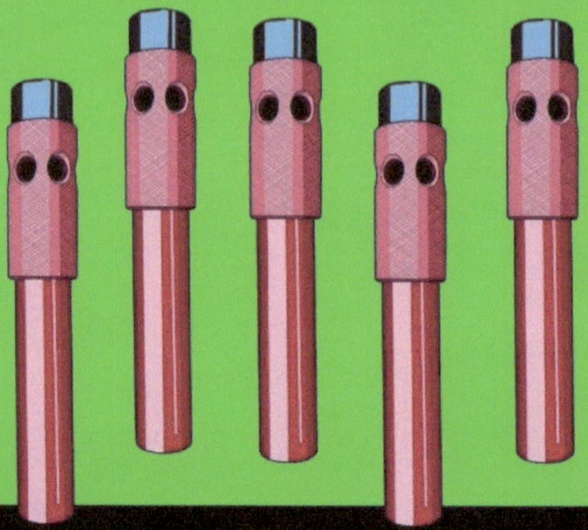

five automatic pistol grip nozzels

5

Can you find the nozzel with two tips?

What color is the smooth bore nozzel?

five distributing barrel nozzels

five forestry nozzels

five smooth bore nozzels

How many smokejumper's parachutes are open?

6

Which airplanes point right?

six smokejumpers

six "jumper" planes

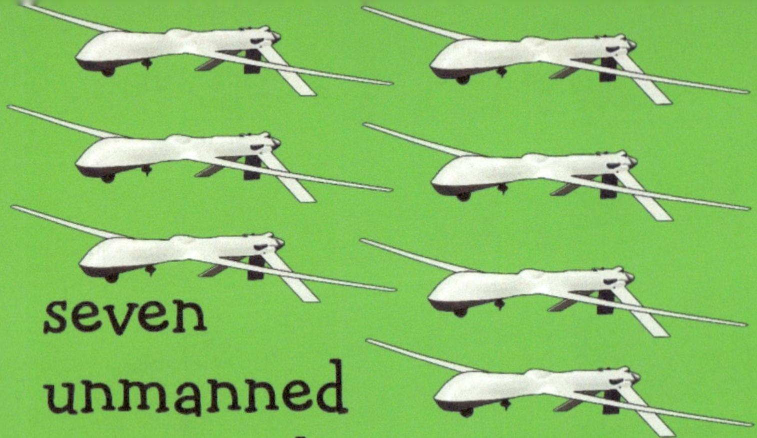

seven unmanned aerial vehicles

seven line packs

Can you find the small line packs?

What image is a "UAV?"

seven fire shelters

seven firefighters

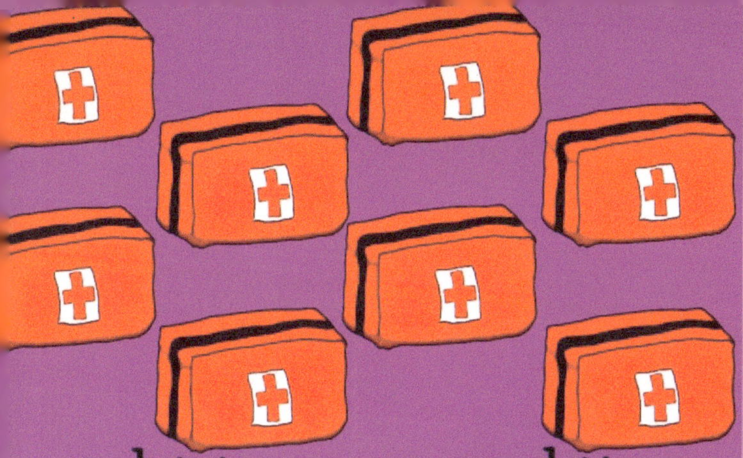

eight ten-person kits

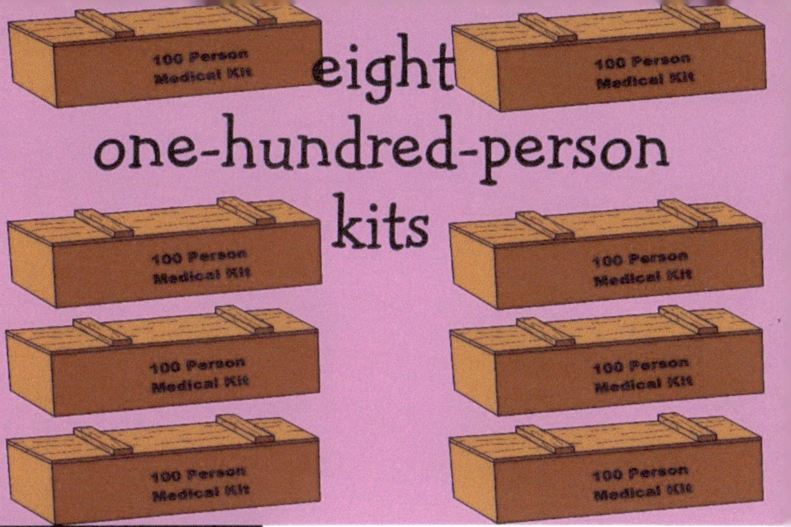

eight one-hundred-person kits

Can you find your first-aid kit?

8

What color is the one-hundred person kit?

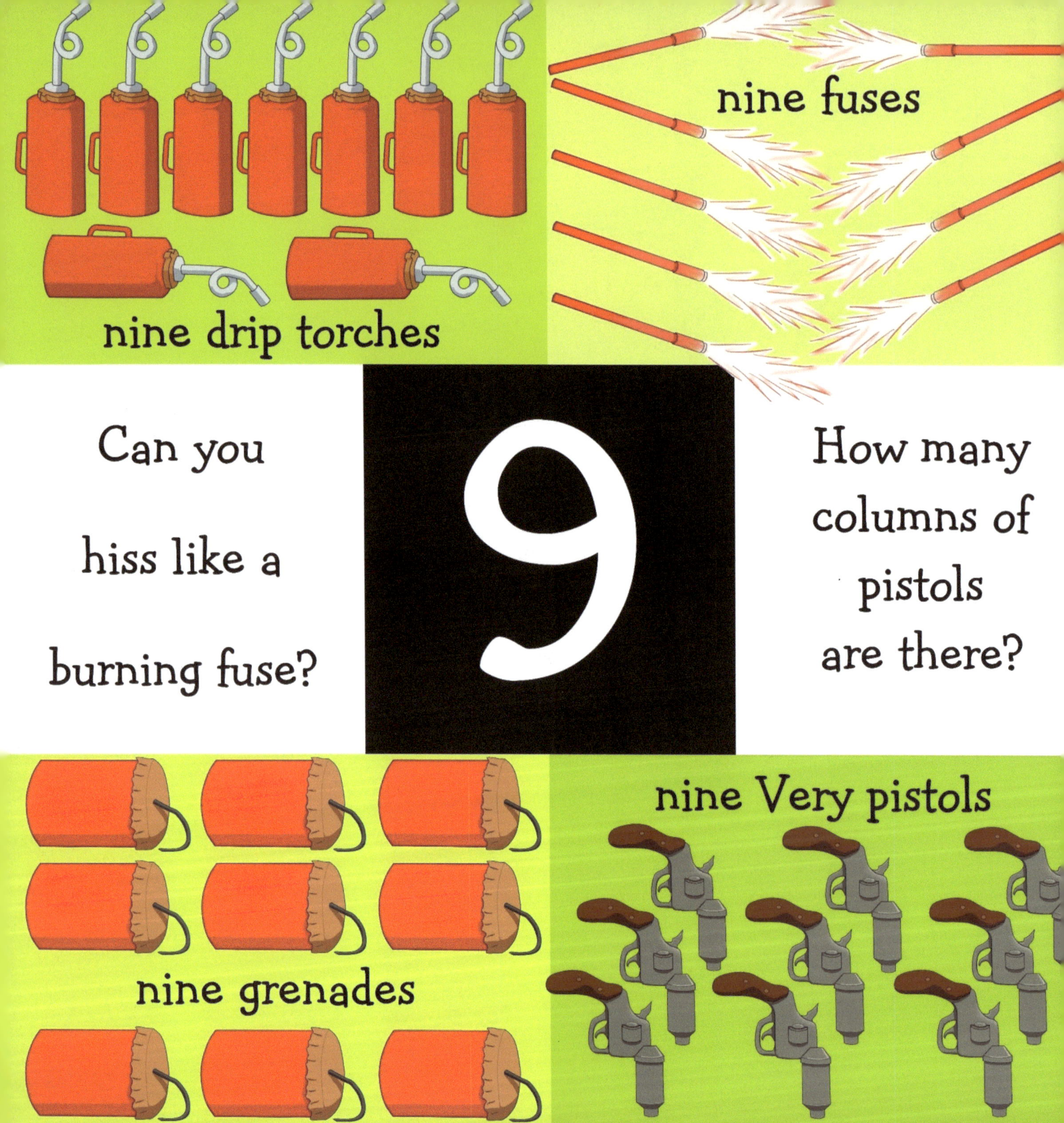
nine drip torches
nine fuses
Can you
hiss like a
burning fuse?
9
How many
columns of
pistols
are there?
nine grenades
nine Very pistols

Can you use your arms like a compass and point North?

How many rows of maps are there?

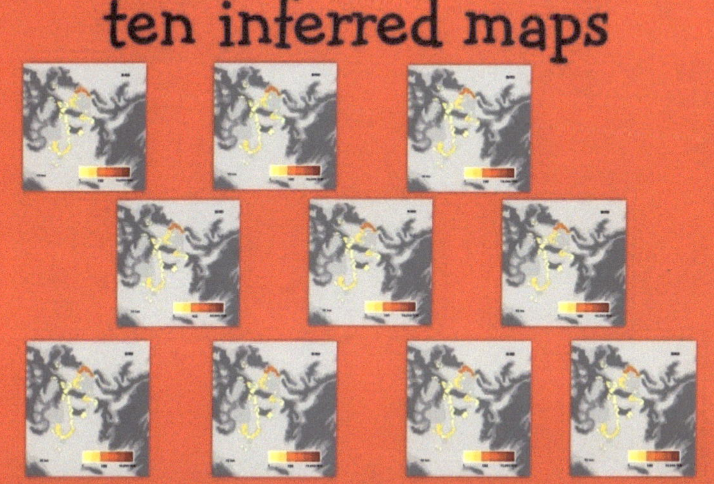

eleven
reducers

eleven
ball shut-off valves

Can you find the appliance with two valves?

What color is the "toy hose" ball shut-off?

twelve pumps

How many red pumps can you see?

What sound does a pump make?

twelve foot valves

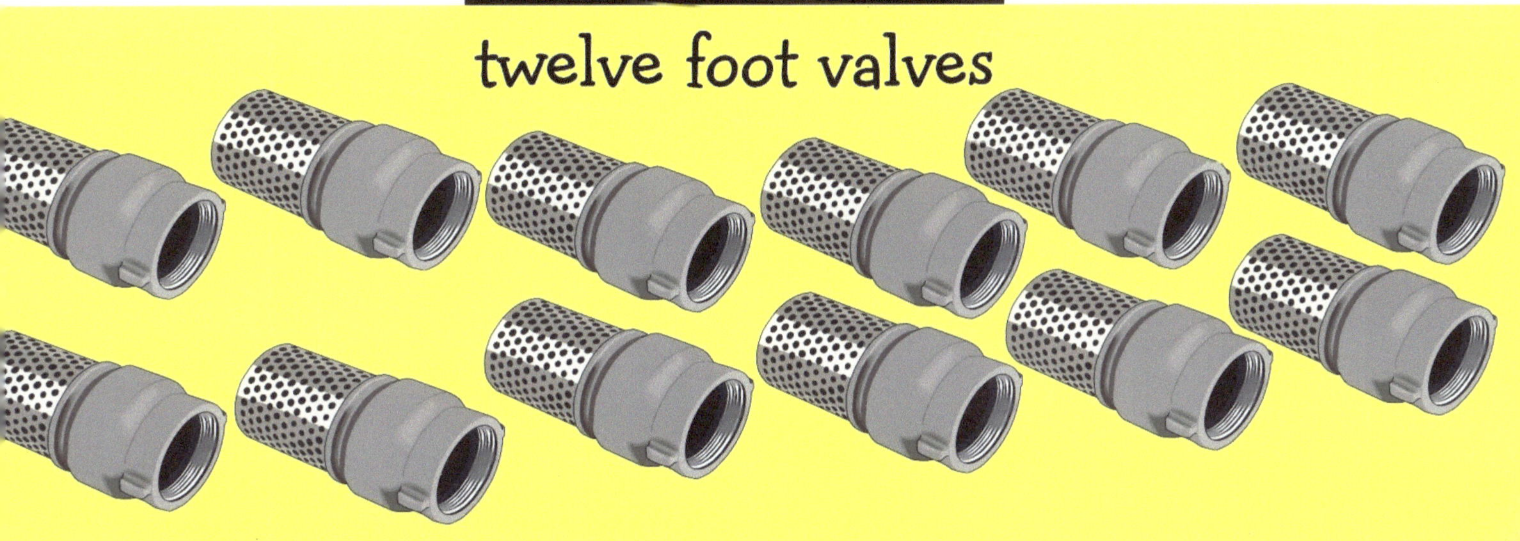

thirteen rouge hoes

Can you pretend to dig with a hoe?

13

What color is the bladder bag?

thirteen bladder bags

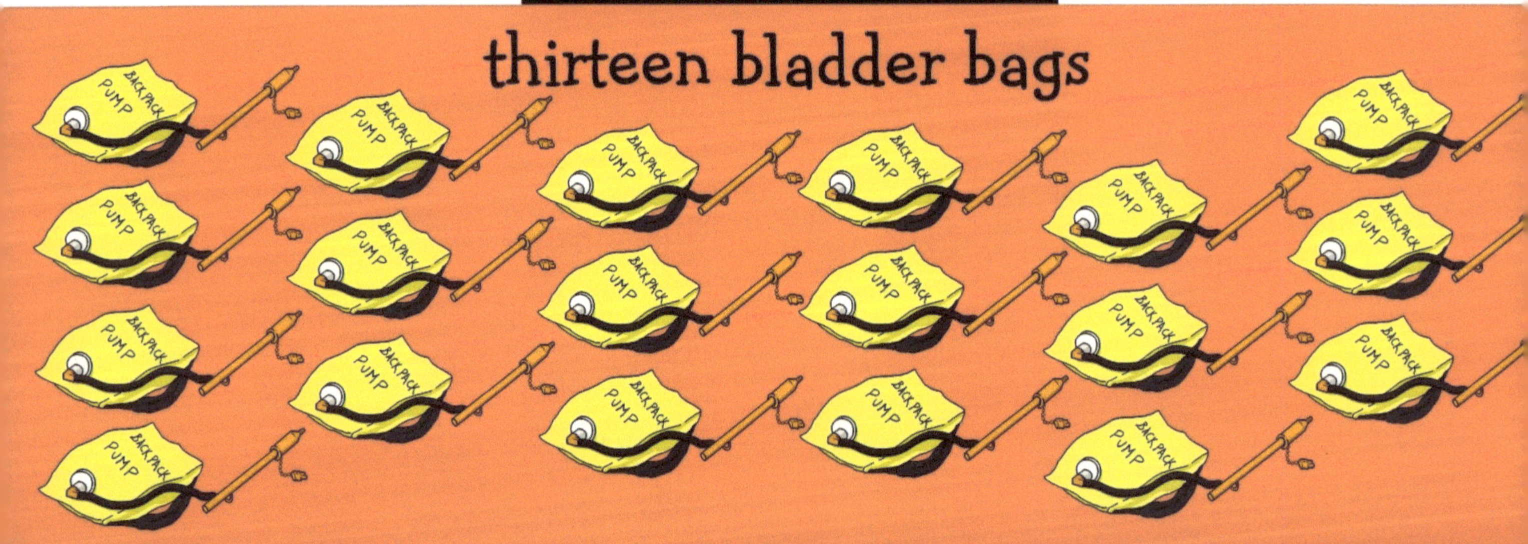

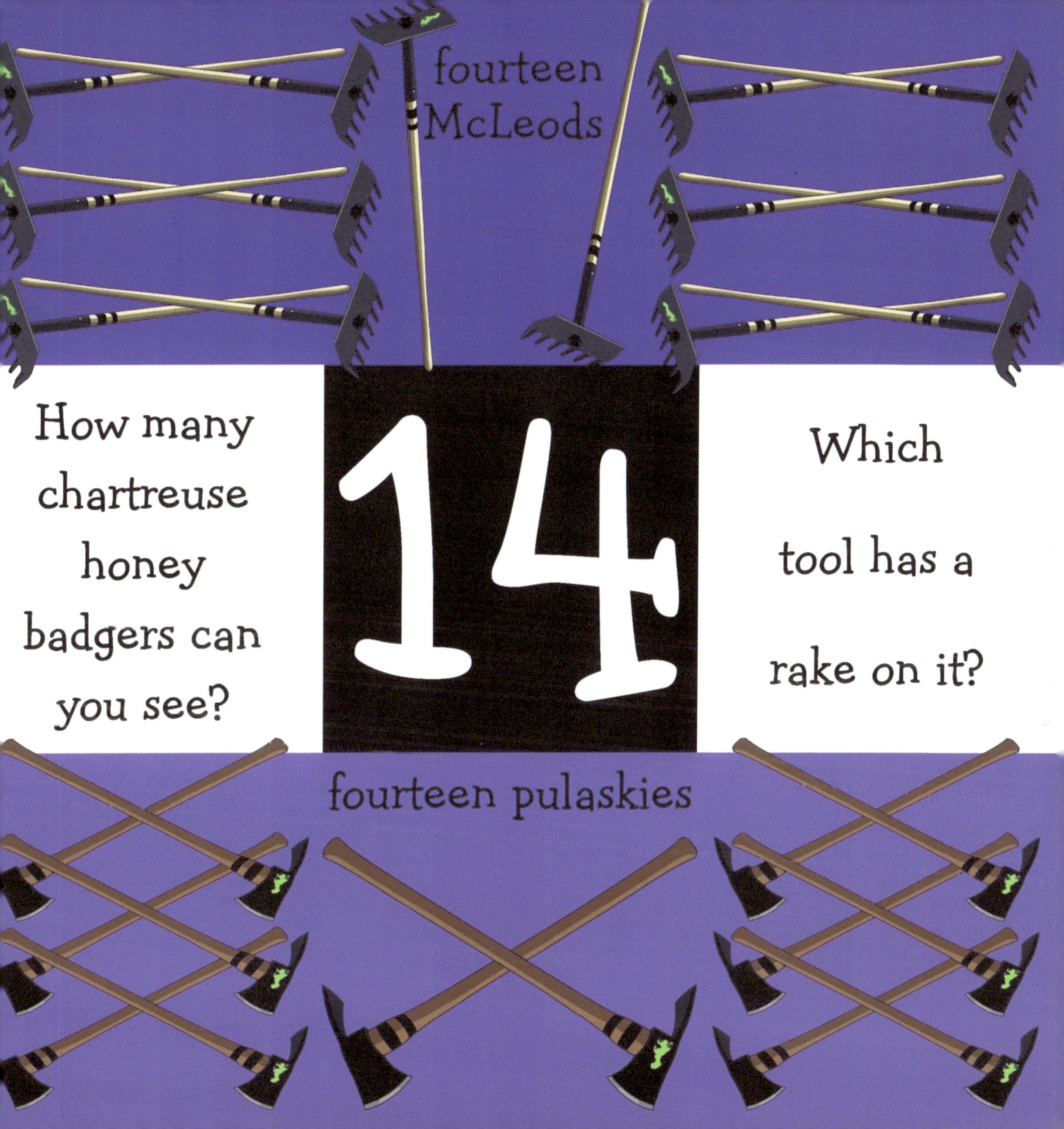
fourteen McLeods
How many chartreuse honey badgers can you see?
14
Which tool has a rake on it?
fourteen pulaskies

fifteen petrol Jerrycans

Where do

do you get

petrol?

What

Jerrycan is

colored blue?

fifteen water Jerrycans

sixteen rhinos

Can you find the orange honey badger?

16

Where do you keep your shovel?

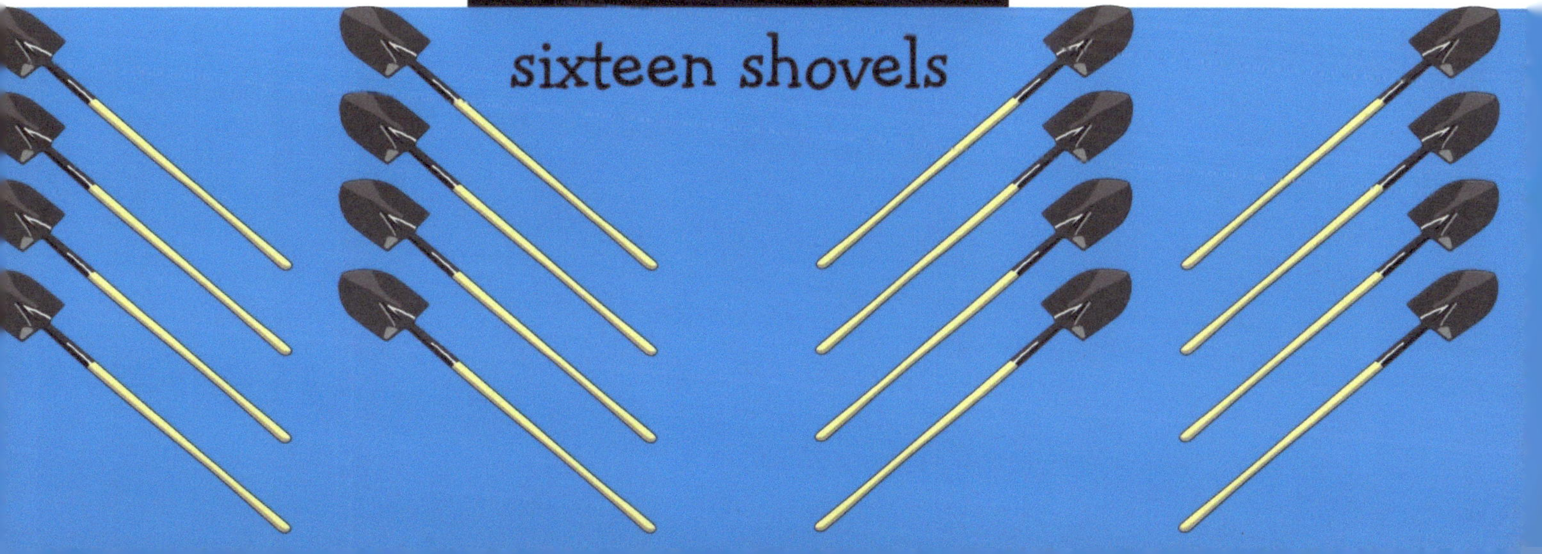

sixteen shovels

seventeen McLaskis

Which tool has a pick?

Which tool has red striping?

seventeen combis

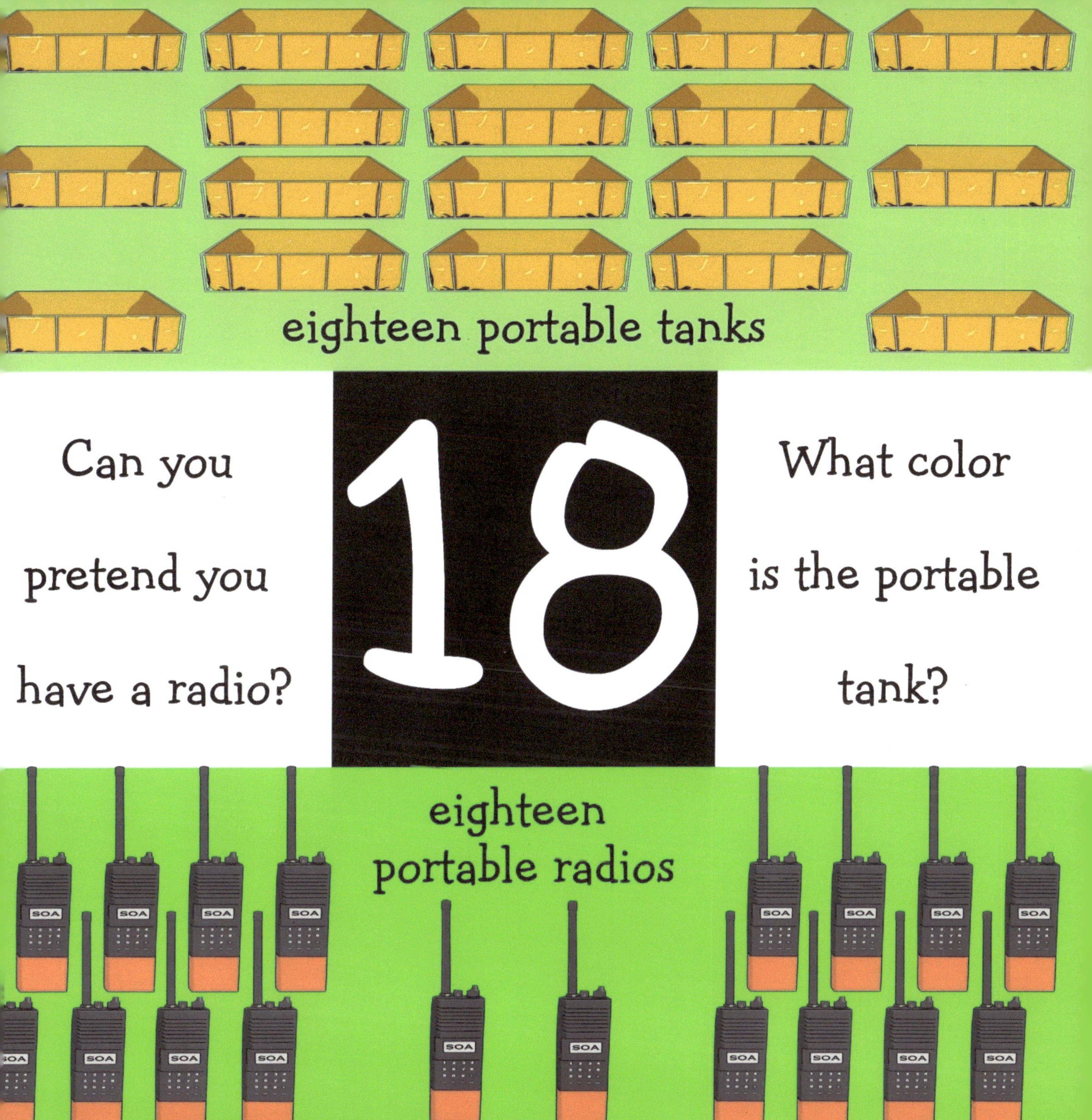
eighteen portable tanks
Can you pretend you have a radio?
18
What color is the portable tank?
eighteen portable radios
SOA

nineteen rolls of hose

Do you have a backpack?

What color is the hose pack?

nineteen hose packs

twenty firefighters

Can you pick 5 modules to make your Task Force?

20

What color are the firefighter's pants?

twenty modules

1	2	3	4	5
one	two	three	four	five
11	12	13	14	15
eleven	twelve	thirteen	fourteen	fiftee
21	22	23	24	25
twenty-one	twenty-two	twenty-three	twenty-four	twenty-fiv

6	7	8	9	10
six	seven	eight	nine	ten
16	17	18	19	20
sixteen	seventeen	eighteen	nineteen	twenty
26	27	28	29	30
venty-six	twenty-seven	twenty-eight	twenty-nine	thirty

Be sure to check this book title, *Wildland Firefighting A,B,C's*, by this author.

You can find this title in both printed and e-book formats.

ABOUT THE AUTHOR

Anthony Monterroso has an extensive background serving his country. He served in the United States Air Force. After becoming certified as an Emergency Medical Technician, he began working for private ambulance service companies. Committed to serving his community and country, he began working as a wildland firefighter (forestry technician.) Anthony Monterroso continues to serve as a firefighter.

CPSIA information can be obtained
at www.ICGtesting.com
Printed in the USA
LVHW071206251118
598196LV00013B/1473/P
* 9 7 8 1 5 4 2 5 9 9 6 9 6 *